IRISH FOLK SONGS
COLLECTION

24 TRADITIONAL FOLK SONGS FOR INTERMEDIATE LEVEL PIANO SOLO

T0071444

ARRANGED BY JUNE ARMSTRONG

ISBN 978-1-4950-9487-3

HAL•LEONARD®
7777 W. BLUEMOUND RD. P.O. BOX 13819 MILWAUKEE, WI 53213

In Australia contact:
Hal Leonard Australia Pty. Ltd.
4 Lentara Court
Cheltenham, Victoria, 3192 Australia
Email: ausadmin@halleonard.com.au

Visit Hal Leonard Online at
www.halleonard.com

PREFACE

Alfred Percival Graves, the Irish poet, was of the opinion that Irish airs seem well-nigh inexhaustible. It has been a delight delving into this vast fund of material, revisiting many of my old favourites and discovering new and enchanting melodies, in making my selection for this collection of Irish folk songs from the rich and diverse heritage of Irish music. I was lucky to have lived in Belfast during the 1970s and to hear The Chieftans, Planxty and Clannad in concert. Some of the pieces I have chosen I first heard at those concerts. I also wished to discover music which was new to me and there are tunes included in the collection which I had never heard before: The Gartan Mother's Lullaby, My Love is an Arbutus, Huish the Cat, That Night in Bethlehem, Squire Parsons, As I Walked Out One Morning and Blind Mary. I would like to express an enormous amount of gratitude to Séamus Quinn for his advice on all matters traditional and for sharing his inexhaustible fund of knowledge with me, and also to John McParland for his generous and untiring expertise on matters of musical finesse. I am greatly indebted to Jennifer Linn for giving me this opportunity to create these arrangements, which come right from the heart and which have been such a joy to engage with.

PROFILE

June Armstrong was born in 1951. She studied music at Queen's University Belfast. She lived in Upstate New York for six years from 1977, where her two sons were born. On returning to Belfast she began a lifelong love affair with teaching the piano. Over the past eight years she has written 13 collections of atmospheric and descriptive piano music for all levels, which are designed to engage the imagination and promote technical development. Her compositions are published by Pianissimo *pp* Publishing. Her music has been selected by major examination boards, and the Contemporary Music Centre, Ireland's national archive for new music.

TABLE OF CONTENTS

NOTES ON THE IRISH FOLK SONGS

MY LOVE IS AN ARBUTUS (COOLA SHORE) (PAGE 6)

The arbutus is an evergreen tree with bell-shaped white or pink flowers and red, strawberry-like fruits in autumn. The tune is probably from County Cavan in Ulster.

> "My love's an arbutus
> By the borders of Lene,
> So slender and shapely In her girdle of green;"

BUNCLODY (PAGE 8)

This very simple melody, like so many Irish tunes, can be found with many variants, but I have chosen here to use this very affecting and unadorned rendering. Bunclody is a small town on the River Slaney in Wexford.

DOWN BY THE SALLEY GARDENS (GORT NA SAILEÁN) (PAGE 9)

The poem by W.B. Yeats was inspired by a half-remembered song by an old peasant woman from Ballisodare in County Sligo. Herbert Hughes subsequently set the verses to the tune "The Maid of the Mourne Shore" in 1909.

> "Down by the salley gardens my love and I did meet;
> She passed the salley gardens with little snow-white feet.
> She bid me take love easy, as the leaves grow on the tree;
> But I, being young and foolish, with her would not agree."

COURTIN' IN THE KITCHEN (PAGE 10)

This lively song is all about the perils of courtship. The unfortunate young man ends up in jail.

> "Come single belle and beau, unto me now pay attention,
> Don't ever fall in love, it's the divil's own invention.
> For once I fell in love with a maiden so bewitchin',
> Miss Henrietta Bell, down in Captain Kelly's kitchen."

I'LL TELL MY MA (PAGE 12)

This infectious tune almost certainly originated as a children's skipping song. The most popular view of where it originates is Belfast with the chorus line of "She is handsome, she is pretty, She is the Belle of Belfast City", but many other towns and city substitute their own name. It is also known as "The Boys Won't Leave the Girls Alone."

BALLINDERRY (PAGE 14)

Edward Bunting first published this sad love song in 1840. It tells of a girl and her love, sitting on bonny Rams Island, but ends with a lament, as the ship carrying her love, has "sunk forever beneath the sea".

THE GARTAN MOTHER'S LULLABY (PAGE 16)

Herbert Hughes collected this intensely beautiful Irish melody in Donegal in 1903 and published it in 1904 in 'The Songs of Uladh (Ulster)'. The song is a lullaby, sung by a mother from the parish of Gartan in County Donegal. The song refers to a number of figures in Irish mythology.

> "Sleep O babe, for the red bee hums
> The silent twilight's fall"

DOWN AMONG THE DITCHES O (PAGE 17)

This lively jig comes from what is probably the earliest collection of Irish music preserved in manuscript, dating from 1770-1800. It was compiled by Pádraig Ó Néill, a piper living near Carrick-on-Suir who was known as 'the merry miller'.

THE CASTLE OF DROMORE (THE OCTOBER WINDS) (PAGE 18)

The very atmospheric Castle of Dromore, also known as The October Winds, is one of the oldest extant Irish songs. In it, a child is lulled to sleep, with a prayer for safety against wild weather and Clann Eoin's wild Banshee.

Slieve Gallion Braes (page 20)

This beautiful lament is a song of regret and of emigration. Slieve Gallion is a mountain on the eastern edge of the Sperrins in County Londonderry.

> "I was thinking on those flowers, all doomed to decay,
> That bloom around ye, bonny, bonny, Slieve Gallion Braes."

The Londonderry Air (Danny Boy) (page 22)

The "Londonderry Air" was first published by George Petrie in1855. It was given to him by Miss Jane Ross of Limavady in County Londonderry. There is much mystery surrounding the origins of the tune and it is believed to have evolved from an older Irish air, "The Young Man's Dream." In 1912, Frederick Weatherly added the words of "Danny Boy" to the melody after his sister-in-law gave him the tune that she heard in Colorado during the Gold Rush. Astonishingly, Weatherly had already written the words of Danny Boy before he had ever seen the music.

Rocky Road to Dublin (page 24)

This infectious slip jig is a 19th century ballad regaling the travels of a man, setting off from his home town of Tuam (where he left the girls of Tuam sad and broken hearted) and travelling to Dublin (a-frightenin' all the dogs, on the rocky road to Dublin) and chronicles all his adventures on his way to Liverpool.

Carrickfergus (page 26)

The origins of the lovely tune Carrickfergus are unclear. It is thought to have been based on a Gaelic song dating from the 18th century. It is a heart-rending song of regret and lost opportunity.

My Lagan Love (page 28)

This exquisite Irish melody and "The Gartan Mother's Lullaby" were collected by Herbert Hughes in Donegal in 1903. The Lagan referred to in the title is most probably an area of farming land between Donegal and Derry. Others maintain that it is the Lagan River that flows through Belfast (and is very close to where I live).

Huish the Cat (page 30)

Francis O'Neill published this single jig in the Dance Music of Ireland in 1907. I believe that "Huish the Cat" means shoo the cat.

The Fairy Woman of Lough Leane (Sí-bhean Locha Léin) (page 32)

Lough Leane is the largest of the three lakes of Killarney. It means the lake of learning, possibly a reference to a monastery on Innisfallen, an island in the lake. The melody is hauntingly beautiful.

The Coolin (An Chúilfhionn) (page 34)

"The Coolin" is considered one of the most beautiful of all Irish airs and it probably dates from the 17th century. It means the fair-haired lady.

The Cliffs of Doneen (page 36)

Jack McAuliffe from County Kerry wrote the words of this lovely ballad about emigration. It describes the beautiful cliffs around Doneen Point near Beale in Kerry. I have read that the music was written afterwards by a local musician, making it unique in this collection.

Squire Parsons (page 38)

This gracefully elegant melody was written by the blind harper Turlough O'Carolan (1670-1738). Many of O'Carolan's tunes were named in honour of patrons whom he entertained and who supported him.

Kitty of Coleraine (page 40)

The earliest printing of this tune appears to be in Kerr's Merry Melodies in the Irish jig section (c. 1886). I know nothing else about the origins of this tune, but the tune itself I have known since I was a child. My family home is in Coleraine in Co. Londonderry, so I had to include it.

That Night in Bethlehem (Don Oíche Úd i mBeithil) (page 41)

This stunningly simple and affecting melody is a rare example of an Irish Christmas Carol. It would have been sung in Gaelic.

As I Walked Out One Morning (page 42)

This optimistic sounding air from County Wexford was first published by George Petrie in 1855 and belies the full title: As I Walked Out One Morning I Heard a Dismal Cry.

Blind Mary (Máire Dhall) (page 43)

William Forde in his Encyclopedia attributes this wistful melody to the blind harper Turlough O'Carolan. Although it is not stylistically consistent with his music (which was greatly influenced by the Italian music of the Baroque era–particularly Vivaldi and Geminiani), it has been mooted that he may have written it in the style of the harper Máire Dhall as a tribute.

Follow Me Up to Carlow (page 44)

In 1580, in Glen Malure in Co. Wicklow, Fiach MacHugh O'Byrne overthrew the forces of Queen Elizabeth I under Lord Gre de Wilton. The victory is commemorated in this stirring song. It is reputed to have been played as a marching tune by the pipers of Fiach MacHugh.

> "Up with halberd, out with sword
> On we'll go for by the Lord,
> Fiach MacHugh has given the word
> Follow me up to Carlow."

My Love Is an Arbutus
(Coola Shore)

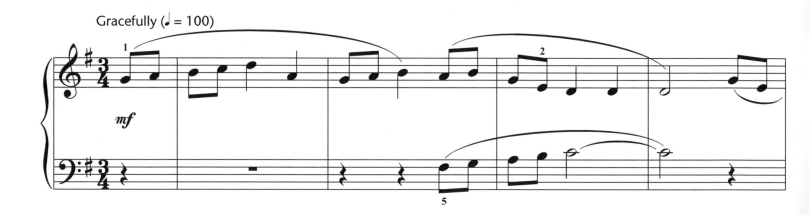

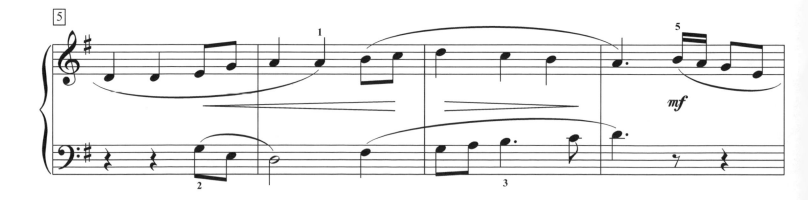

BUNCLODY

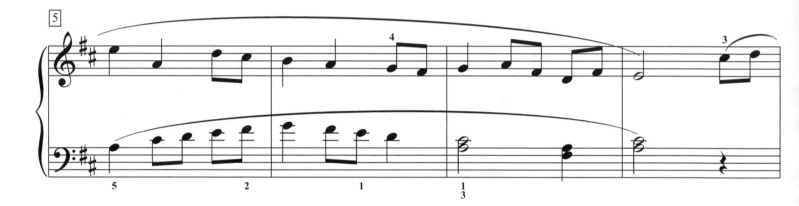

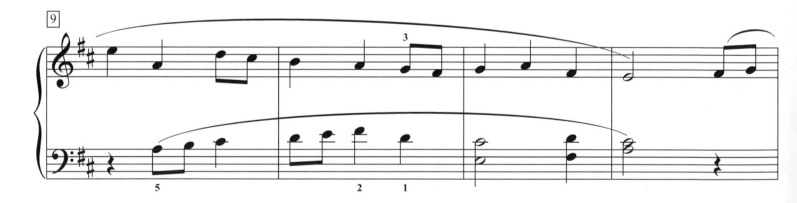

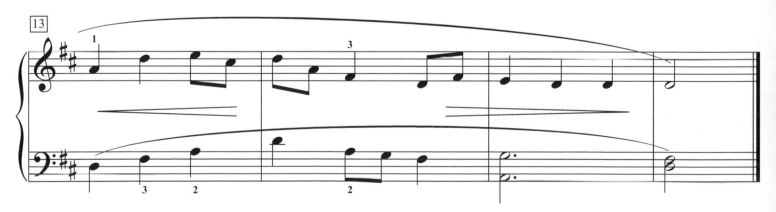

DOWN BY THE SALLEY GARDENS
(GORT NA SAILEÁN)

Tenderly (♩ = 84)

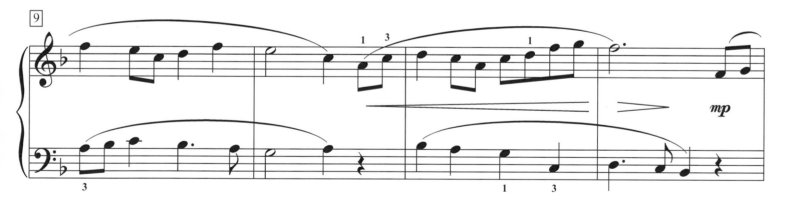

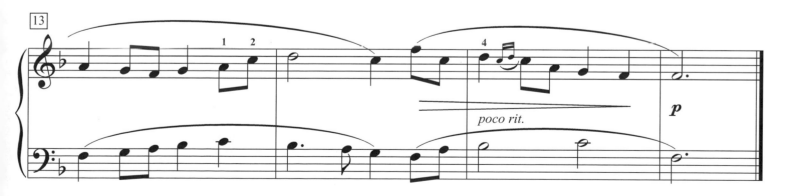

Courtin' in the Kitchen

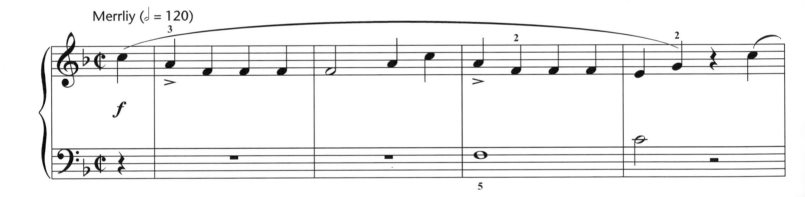

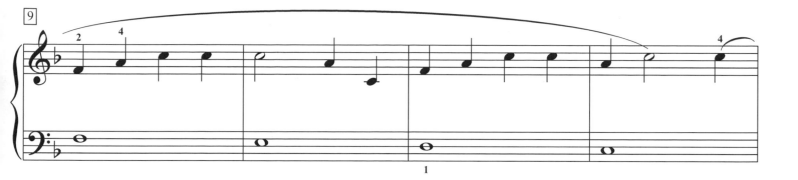

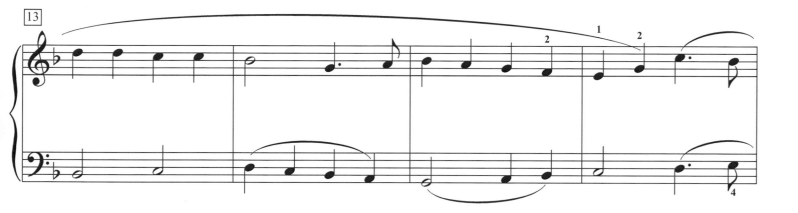

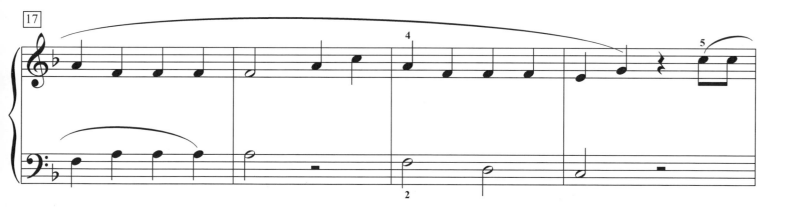

I'LL TELL MY MA

Cheekily ($\dot{}$ = 100)

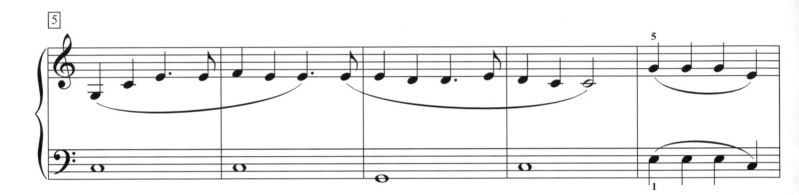

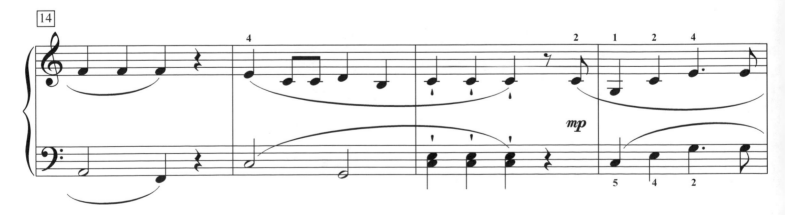

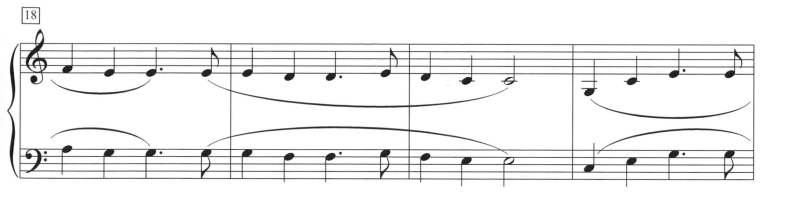

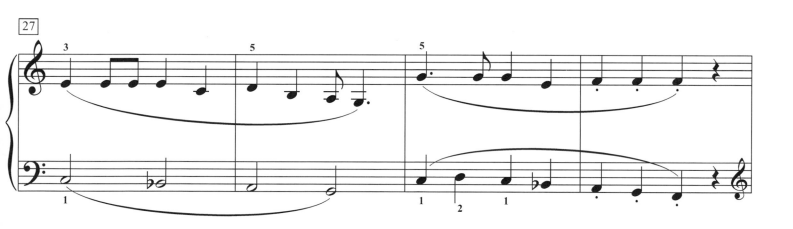

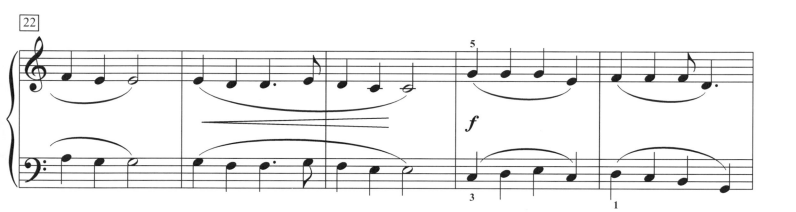

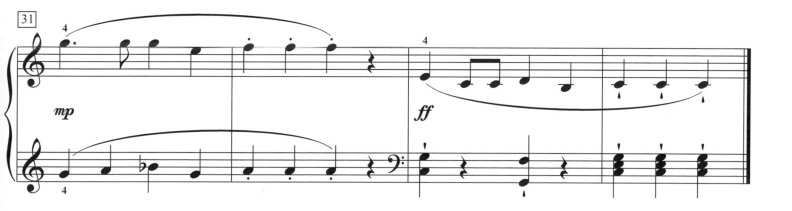

BALLINDERRY

Wistfully (♩ = 116)

mp

With pedal
5 4 2

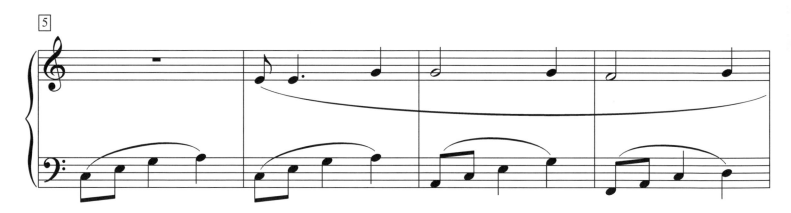

5

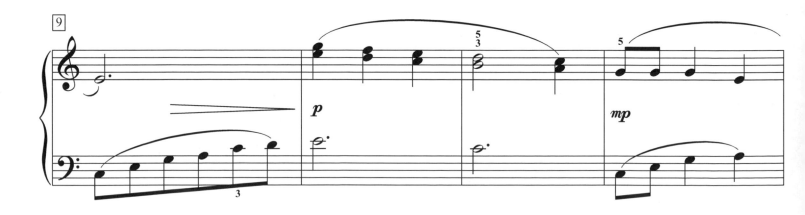

9

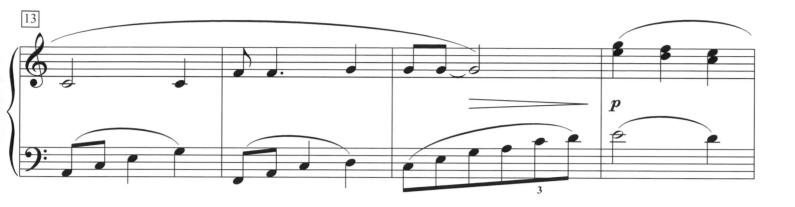

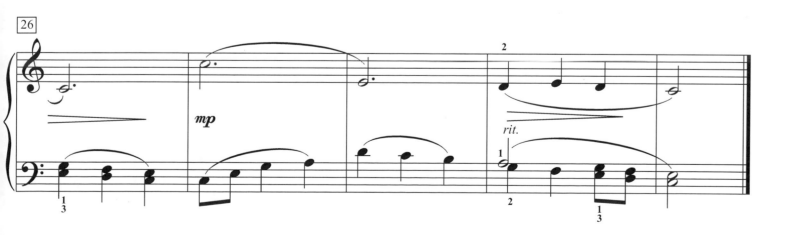

THE GARTAN MOTHER'S LULLABY

Tenderly (♩. = 52)

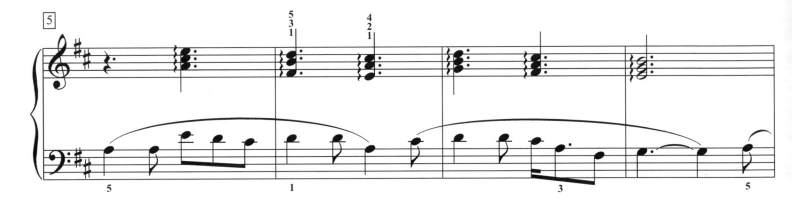

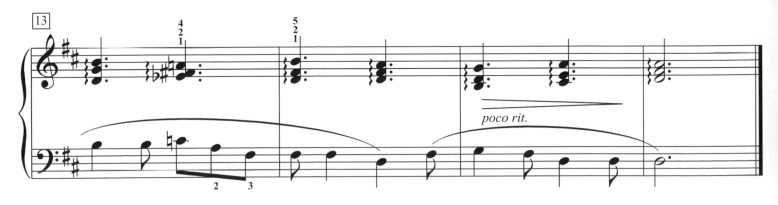

Down Among the Ditches O

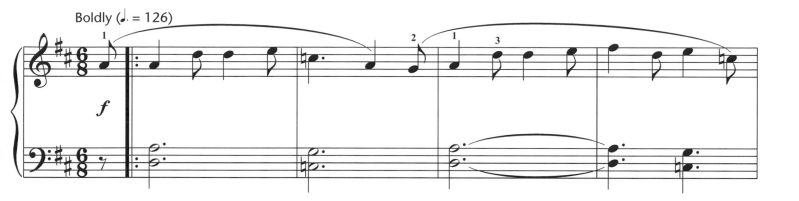

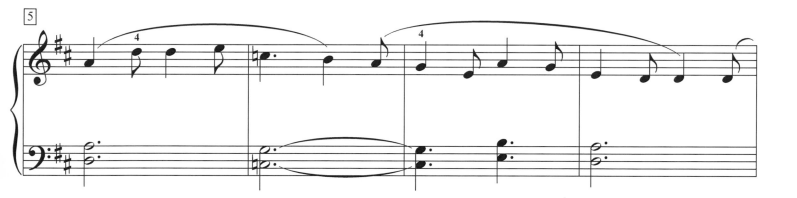

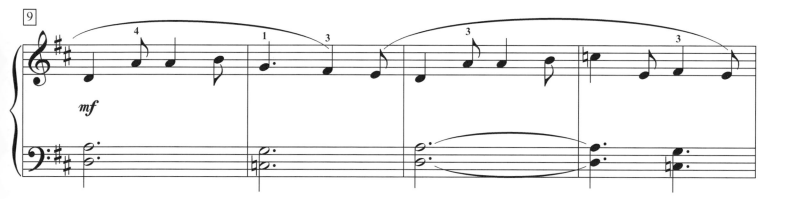

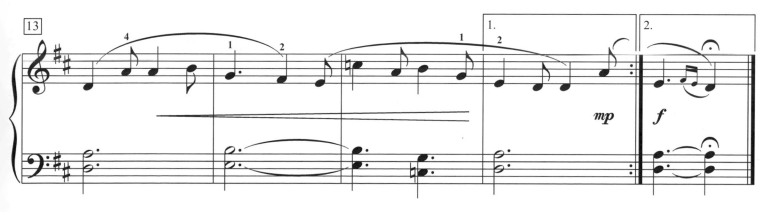

THE CASTLE OF DROMORE
(THE OCTOBER WINDS)

With pedal

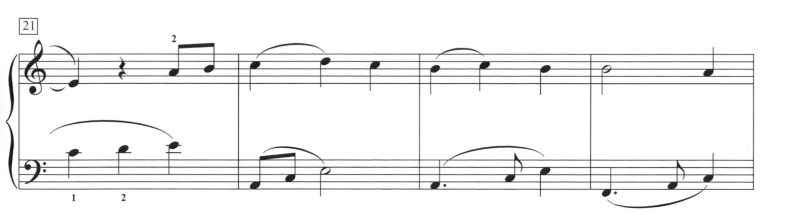

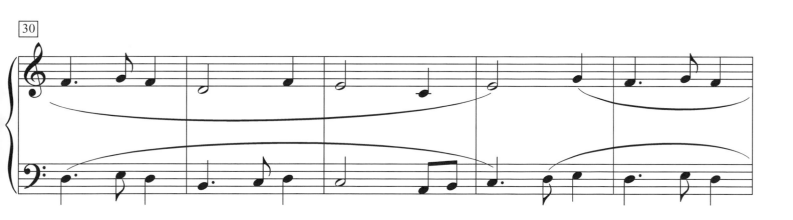

SLIEVE GALLION BRAES

With intensity (♩ = 56)

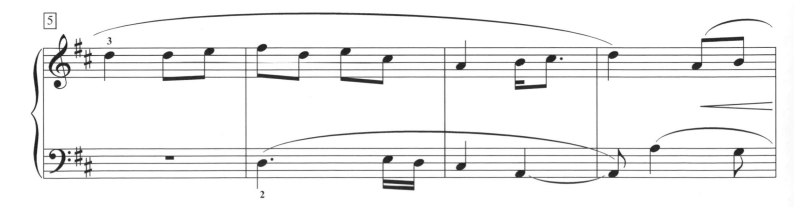

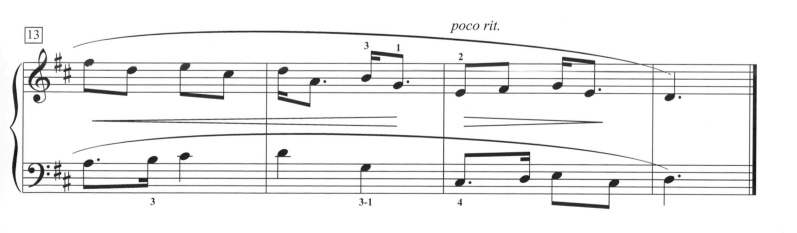

The Londonderry Air
(Danny Boy)

With feeling (♩ = 70)

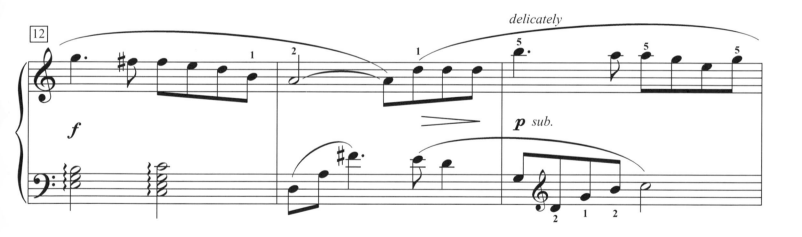

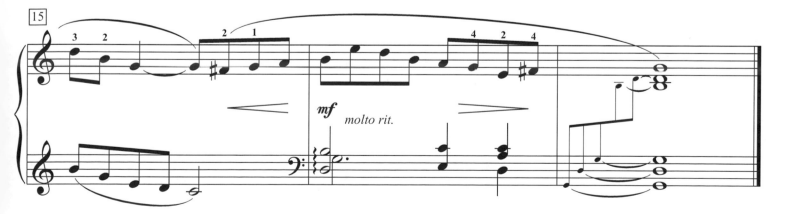

ROCKY ROAD TO DUBLIN

25

CARRICKFERGUS

Longingly (♩ = 76)

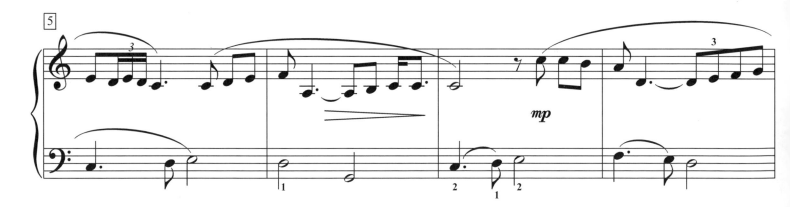

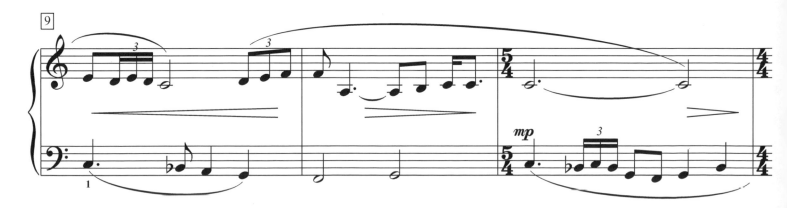

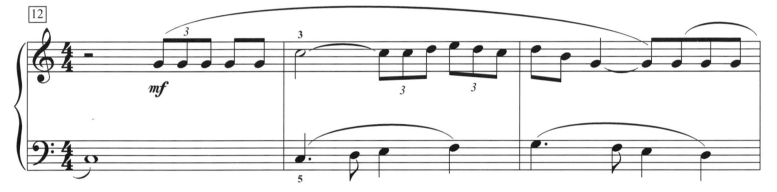

MY LAGAN LOVE

Freely and delicately (♩ = 60)

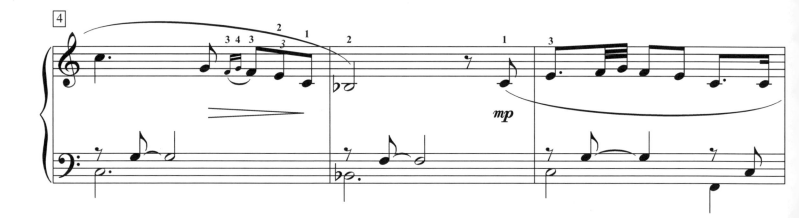

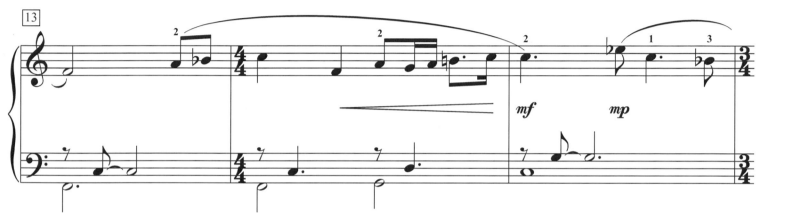

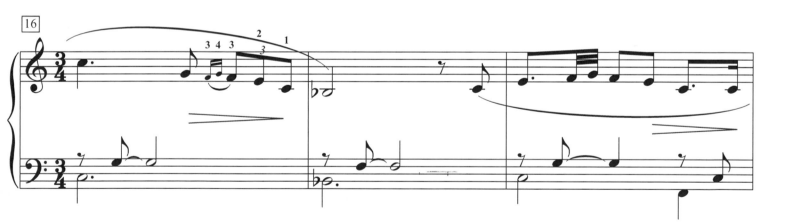

HUISH THE CAT

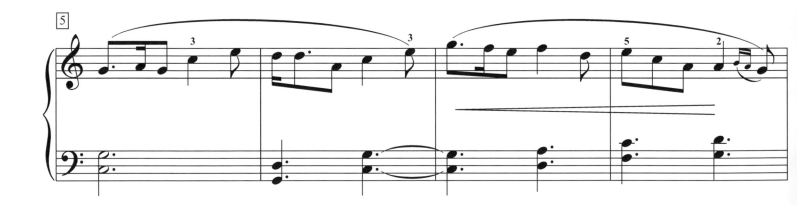

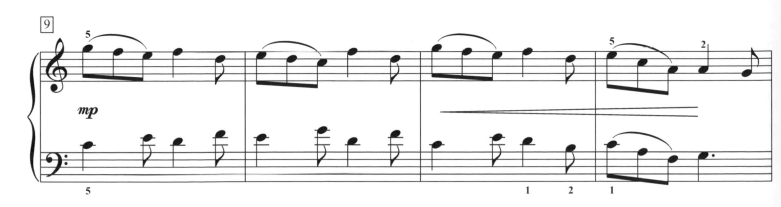

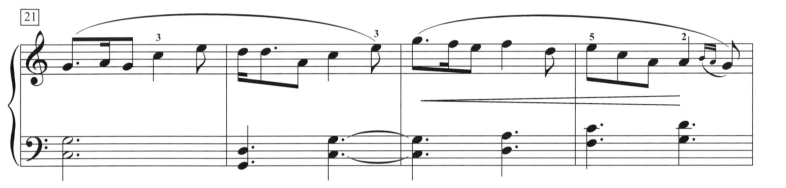

THE FAIRY WOMAN OF LOUGH LEANE
(SÍ-BHEAN LOCHA LÉIN)

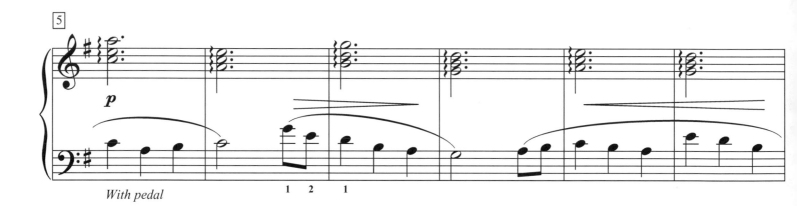

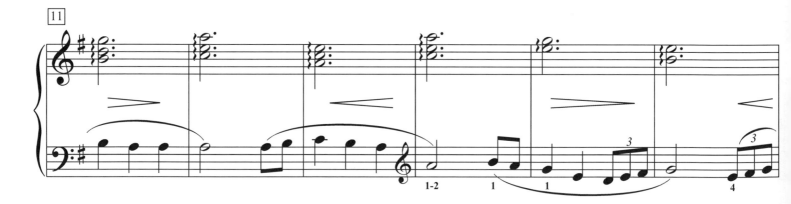

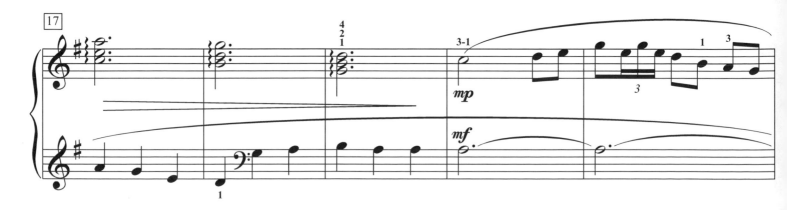

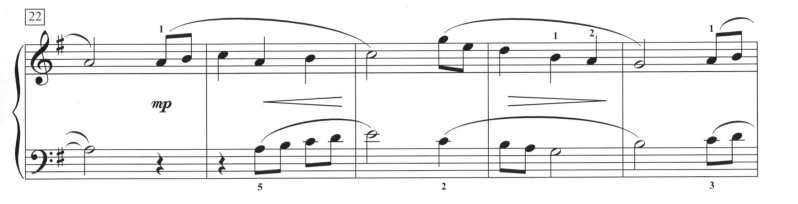

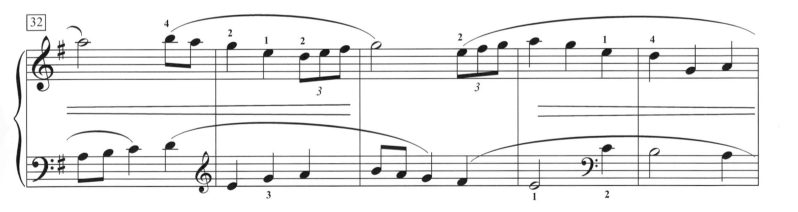

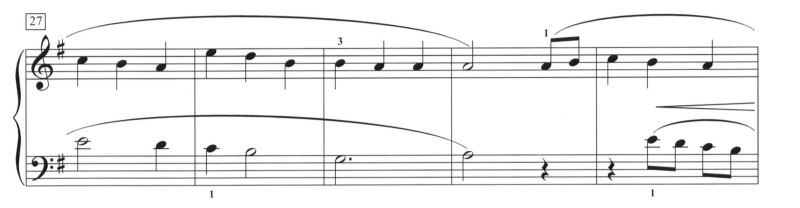

THE COOLIN
(AN CHÚILFHIONN)

Gently (♩ = 60)

With pedal

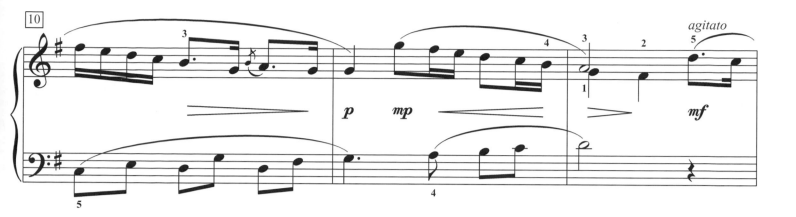

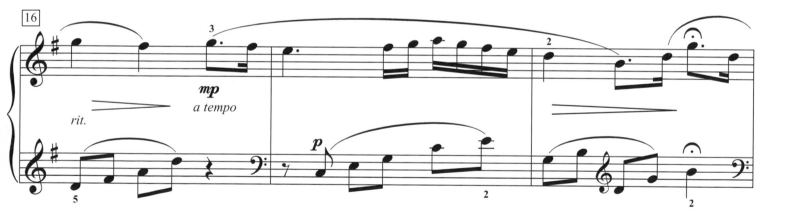

THE CLIFFS OF DONEEN

Wistfully (♩ = 100)

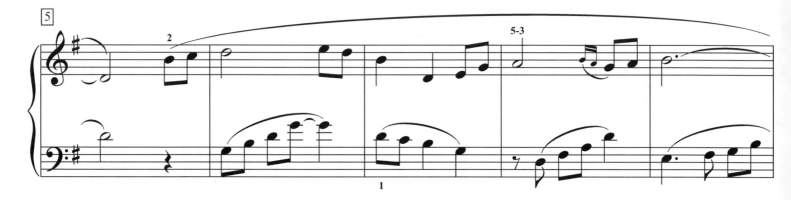

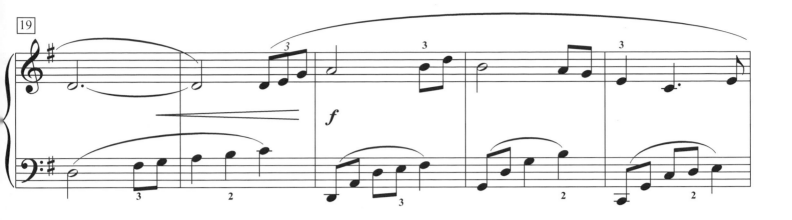

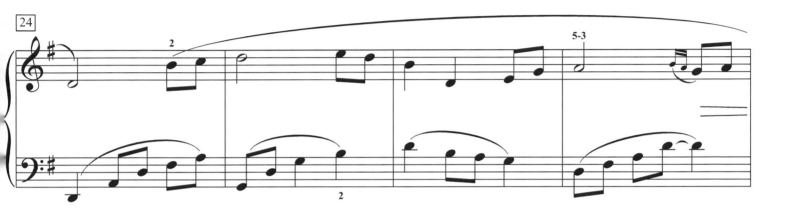

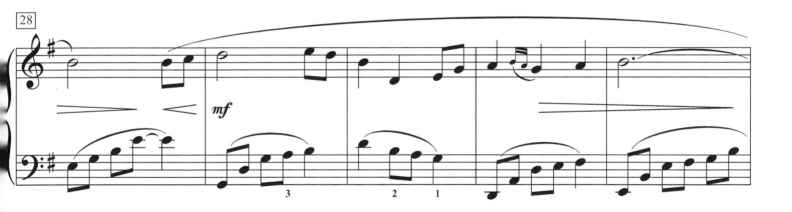

Squire Parsons

By Turlough O'Carolan
Arranged by June Armstrong

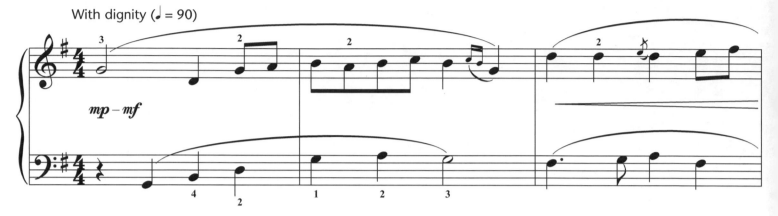

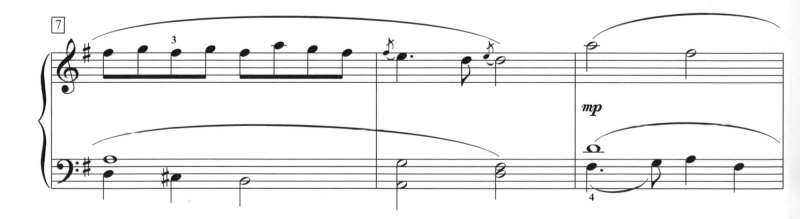

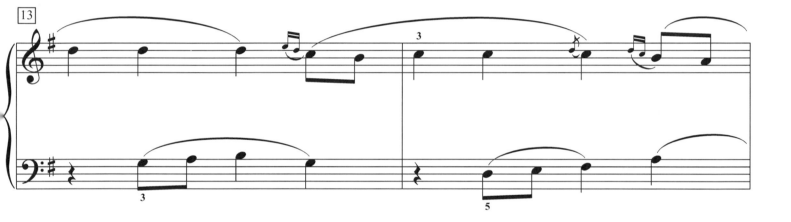

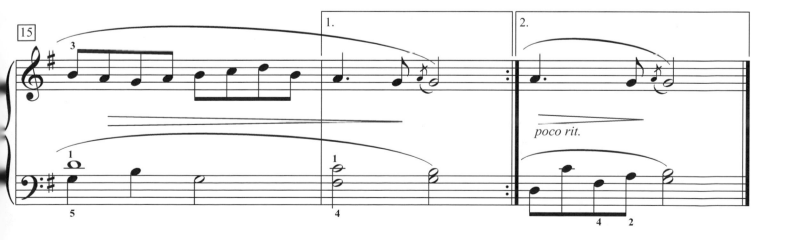

poco rit.

KITTY OF COLERAINE

THAT NIGHT IN BETHLEHEM
(Don Oíche Úd i mBeithil)

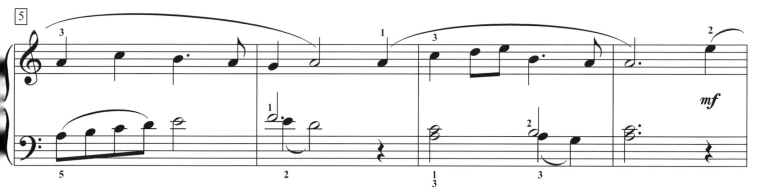

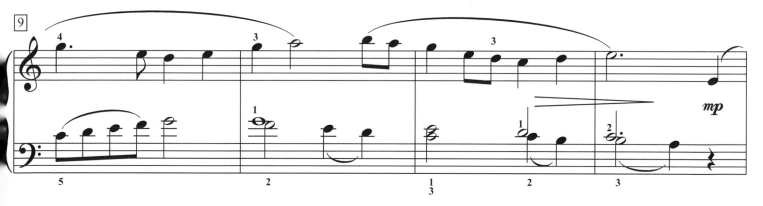

As I Walked Out One Morning

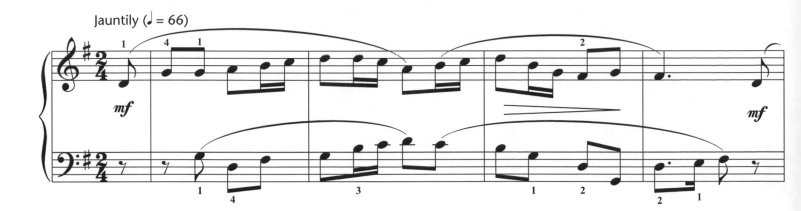

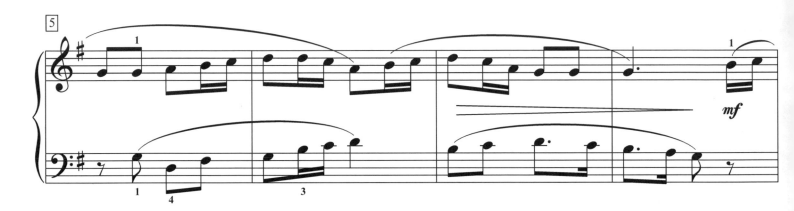

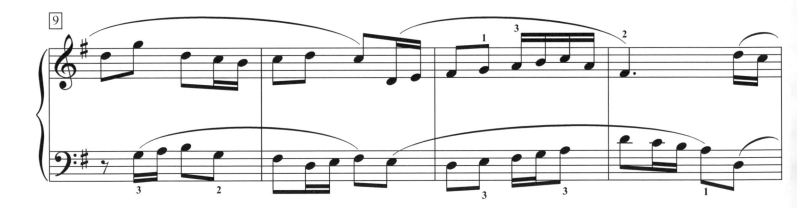

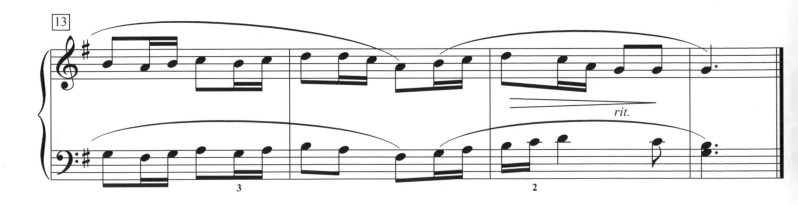

BLIND MARY
(MÁIRE DHALL)

By Turlough O'Carolan
Arranged by June Armstrong

Calmly (♩ = 46)

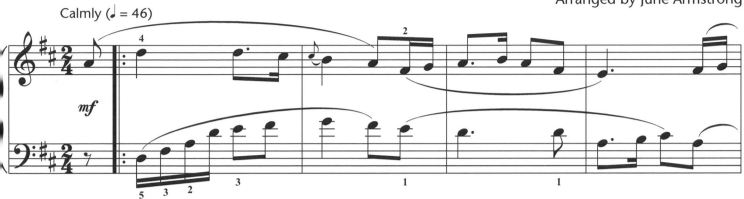

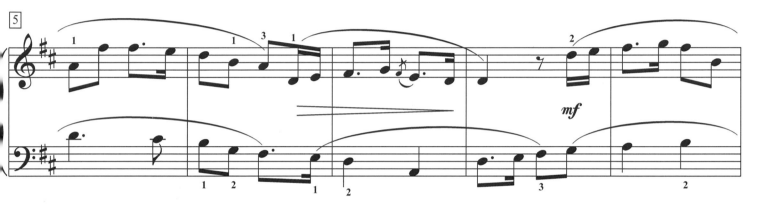

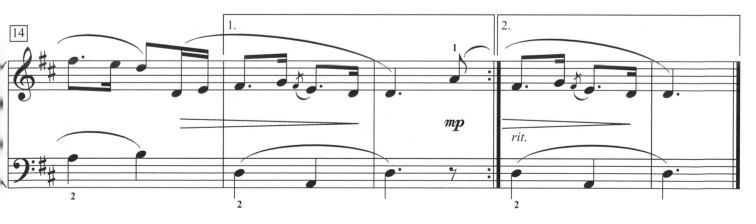

FOLLOW ME UP TO CARLOW

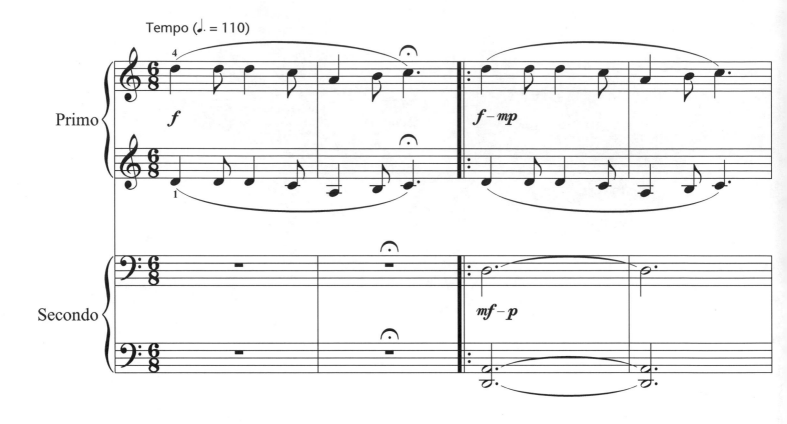

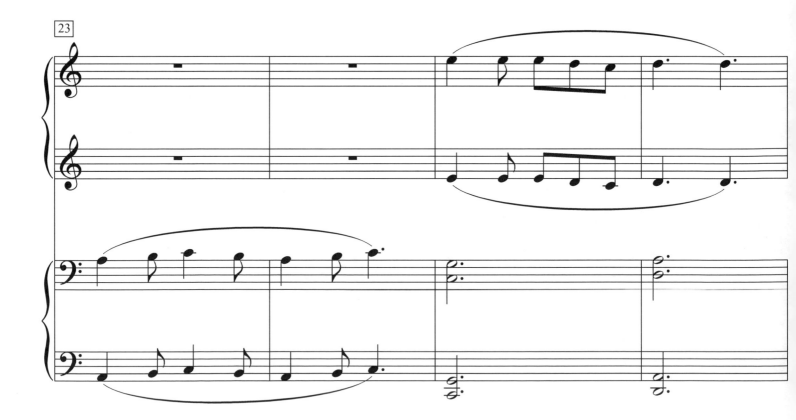

MAP OF IRELAND